MW01252663

THE PERFECT
RING

THE PERFECT
RING

By Lisa Lebowitz Cader

Cader Books

Andrews and McMeel

A Universal Press Syndicate Company
Kansas City

Library of Congress Cataloging-in-Publication Data

Cader, Lisa Lebowitz.
     The perfect ring / by Lisa Lebowitz Cader.
         p.   cm.
     ISBN 0-8362-8038-5 : $9.95
     1. Diamonds—Purchasing.   2. Rings—Purchasing.   I. Title.
TS753.C33   1993
736' .23'0296–dc20   93-28240
                                                                          CIP

COVER SHOT
Photo courtesy of the Diamond Information Center

CONTENTS

Acknowledgments 6
Introduction 9

The Style Guide
A Brief History 14
Diamond Shapes 16
Finding the Right Shape for You 21
Popular Ring Styles 26
Wedding Bands 50

The Buyer's Guide
The Stone 62
The Four C's 64
How to Look at a Diamond 81
Getting Set: Metals and Mounting 88
A Setting Primer 98
Mounting Evidence: Engagement Ring Trends 101
The Purchase: The Fifth C—Cost 107
A Big Diamond Look Without the Big Diamond Price 112
Where to Buy It 116
Antique Rings 123

Appendices
Cleaning Your Ring 138
Resources 140

ACKNOWLEDGMENTS

In the process of researching this book, many people generously shared their time and knowledge with me. My sincere thanks to Ted Mandell and Howard Schwartz at the Diamond Vault for reading the manuscript and giving me their informed opinions; to Joan Boening at James Robinson, my gratitude for educating me about antique rings; to Jonathan Birnbach, president of Wellcut Manufacturers, Inc., for sharing his insights into the diamond business, and for showing me, firsthand, how tools of the trade work; to Paul Phelps, at Osborne-Phelps, a fine jewelry designer in his own right and a great teacher, I'm grateful for the information on mountings and setting metals—complete with step-by-step diagrams to illustrate each point; to Brian Lange, assistant vice president of marketing for Cartier, Inc., a thank you for a tour through Cartier's rich history, past and present; to Roy Albers, senior buyer of diamonds and gemstones for Tiffany & Co., a thank you for explaining the art and science behind the physics of diamonds; to Jeanne Daniel, senior vice president of merchandising for Tiffany & Co., I'm grateful for information on the fine points of ring marketing and styling; to Cheryl Pellegrino, senior account executive at the Diamond Information Center, thank you for the numerous photographs, industry referrals, and advice throughout the making of this book; to Esther Fortunoff, executive vice president of Fortunoff, for invaluable insights into ring buying, and for a lot of plain good sense suggestions; a big thank you to Audrey Bromstead at *JQ* magazine, for beautiful color transparencies; to Russell Shor, senior editor at *JCK* magazine, for most helpful information; to Erin Oates at the Platinum Guild International, for beautiful images and important information; to Tom Yonelunis, CEO of GIA Gem Trade Laboratory, for information on independent gem grading; to Jennifer Herrman, gallery assistant at Aaron Faber, for slides and advice in matching old rings and new; to Brian Ross of Reinstein/Ross, for information on gold and goldsmithing; to Geri Bondanza, Bill Smith, and Michael Bondanza for trend information; to Theresa Boin of Whitney Boin Design Studio, for information and images; to Jennifer Foley, assistant vice president, Sotheby's jewelry department, and Magda Gregorian in Sotheby's public relations for inside information of the buying of rings at auction; to Laura Crimmins of Christie's East for auction information and striking visuals; and to Michael Cader, my partner, best friend, and best editor, who gave me my perfect ring, and without whom this book wouldn't exist, all my appreciation.

INTRODUCTION

≈

The Perfect Ring is a book born of personal experience. When my husband and I began our search for an engagement ring, we quickly discovered that we had more questions than answers. While sales clerks kindly provided advice and "mini-lessons" on how to buy diamonds, and some stores outfitted us with free booklets or pamphlets, we found the information to be confusing, and at times biased. When we asked direct questions about quality and value, some stores replied with vague non-answers that played up the romance of the situation in order to convince us to spend more money than we had budgeted. What we were looking for was sound, objective information, clearly presented—in essence, a gem world equivalent of *Consumer Reports*.

An engagement ring is a significant purchase. And as the experts at the best-known jewelry stores agree, one of the most blind investment purchases couples will ever make. Well over 1.6 million people buy engagement rings each year, at an average price of $1,500 per ring. Although some couples spend less, and others spend significantly more, any way you look at it, it's a lot of money. Particularly if you're not sure what you are doing. We, like other couples, stumbled hesitantly through the issues of choosing a jeweler, buying a diamond, choosing the setting metal and mountings—the number of decisions to be made was surprising—all the while wishing we had some additional guidance.

Along the way we also found that style was a big question. Although I had assumed I would want an emerald-cut diamond, when it came to actually trying rings on, I found that these rectangular-shape stones didn't have enough sparkle for my taste. And I preferred the way round stones looked on my hand. What ensued was a long process of trying rings on at as many local stores as possible—a sizable task in Manhattan!

The result of our search is *The Perfect Ring*. The book demystifies the diamond-buying process for both bride and groom. For women, the largest ring dilemma is one of style. Few brides know what they want, or have any sense of what is available. Ring style is an important factor—after all, you will be wearing this every day for the rest of your life. Part I of *The Perfect Ring* is the quintessential style book of what's current, what's classic, and what's right for you. It features a style compendium that provides color pictures presenting the most popular ring shapes and styles. It also shows diamond ring alternatives, such as jeweled bands and rings that mix precious stones such as sapphires, emeralds, and rubies. And it discusses factors to consider when choosing the shape and look of a ring to assure an intelligent purchase. There are also sections for both men and women on choosing a wedding ring—because with that purchase, the confusion starts all over again.

Part II of *The Perfect Ring* supplies comprehensive information about diamond purchasing, from what to look for in a jeweler to having a diamond appraised for insurance. It discusses the factors that determine a diamond's cost—cut, clarity, carat weight, etc.—but delivers the information in the unique format of: What Jewelers Will Tell You, and What You Should Know. The book contains a lot of information about mountings and setting metals, as well as a section on antique rings and buying rings at auction.

I've also included an important section on getting the

most for your money. Although men still foot the bill, more than 70 percent of couples now shop for a ring together. Each Saturday, at jewelry stores around the nation, tense dramas play out between men and women as the talk turns to price. (Money is always a big issue between partners, and if you want to know how equipped the two of you are to deal with money matters, here's a perfect testing ground.) The good news is most rings can be manufactured at a variety of price points. An accommodating jeweler can help you buy diamonds at a size and of a quality that will fit your budget. Whether for a man shopping solo, a woman looking for the right style, or a couple searching together, *The Perfect Ring* guides you to an educated choice.

Finding the perfect ring for the two of you as a couple is an exciting, but delicate, process. *The Perfect Ring* acknowledges that modern engagements are more complicated than taking Grandma's ring out of the vault and screwing your courage to the kneeling place. It is no secret that the period leading up to the wedding is filled with both joy and stress. *The Perfect Ring* aims to help take some of the anxiety out of that first big step.

THE STYLE GUIDE

A Brief History

Diamonds are the hardest natural substance known to man, and they have become a symbol of love because of this durability, which evokes the unbreakable bond of marriage. It wasn't always that way. Although diamonds were discovered in India in about 1000 B.C., and subsequently invested with mystical symbolism by many cultures, it was centuries later that the Archduke Maximilian of Austria first paired diamonds with betrothal in the ring he gave to Mary of Burgundy in 1475. The royal tradition was embraced by the people and diamonds and engagement rings have been inseparable ever since.

Diamonds are a true miracle of nature. Like coal, candle soot, or the lead of a graphite pencil, a diamond is composed of carbon, a very simple natural element. The difference is that billions of years ago, carbon, in magma deep within the earth's core, was subjected to tremendous heat and pressure that caused it to crystallize. A volcanic eruption took place, forcing the magma through the earth's crust, forming, among other things, the mother lodes of diamonds mined today. In their natural state, diamonds are most commonly eight-sided crystals that resemble the New Age crystal jewelry that has been kicking around this country for the last decade. The earliest diamond rings used the stones in this rough crystalline form. When jewelers developed the first crude cutting techniques, the early cut stones looked like mirrors. They reflected all the light, and had none of the fiery quality of today's stones. As a result, historically, the emphasis was on the settings of rings—elaborate enamel and metal work, as well as inscriptions—rather than the stones.

A confluence of events in the early twentieth century changed all that. In 1870 diamond mines were discovered in Africa, and a suddenly plentiful supply made diamonds available to the middle classes. Diamond-cutting techniques improved. And in 1886, Louis Tiffany devised the six-prong Tiffany setting—a vehicle for showing off the stone's beauty—and the emphasis moved from the setting to the stone itself. The solitaire (a single round brilliant-cut stone) became an instant classic and it is still by far the most popular style.

Diamond Shapes

Square shape or pear shape, these stones don't lose their shape . . .

Diamonds, like people, come in every shape imaginable. But while some body shapes are less elegant than others, there are no stigmas attached to diamond shapes. Most women would agree: They've never met a diamond they didn't like. There are, however, front-runners. More than 75 percent of all diamonds sold are round stones, also called brilliants, because they are more sparkly than the other shapes. Every other shape is called a fancy. The oval, marquise, emerald cut, princess cut (or square), and the pear shape are the better known fancy shapes. Unlike round brilliants, there are no firmly entrenched ideals for fancy shape stones. A pear-shape diamond may be long and thin (more like a Bosc pear), or bottom-heavy—almost shield shape (more like an Anjou). One pear-shape stone may have more fire or brilliance than another, due, in part, to variations in shape. As with so many diamond decisions, it's up to you to decide which shape stone you prefer, and then within those parameters, which permutation is most pleasing.

In addition to the six best-known shapes, shown on the following spread, there are a number of new variations gaining in popularity. They include:

The trillion—A triangular shape stone. Sometimes used as a center stone, it is a very popular accent stone that's challenging tapered baguettes as the favorite to flank a center diamond.

Princess cut or square—A new shape, evolved from the emerald cut, but faceted to produce more brilliance. As with a trillion, it can be used as a center or side stone.

Baguettes—Small rectangular accent stones that are step cut. Often used on the shoulder of a ring to complement a center diamond. Baguettes set end-to-end are a popular choice for Eternity bands.

Tapered Baguettes—A variation of the baguette, these stones are actually slight trapezoids, rather than pure rectangles. In very classic rings tapered baguettes will flank a round center stone. The wider end of the baguette is set next to the center stone, and the slim

The round brilliant. The diamond shape with the most popular appeal. Many couples find this to be the most pleasing shape in terms of fire and brilliance, even though a round stone appears smaller than a fancy-shape stone of comparable size. A round brilliant is characterized by 58 facets.

The marquise, pointed on both ends, has a graceful, elongated shape. Its name pays homage to the marquise Madame de Pompadour.

The pear shape is round on one end and comes to a point at the other end. It is a very elegant shape that is flattering on hands of many shapes and sizes.

The oval is an elegant variation on the round brilliant. One of diamond history's great oval stones is the Koh-i-noor, housed among the Crown Jewels in the Tower of London.

The emerald cut is a chic, understated shape with step-cut facets (literally facets that look like steps) on each of the sides of the rectangle and at the corners. Step-cut stones have less sparkle than brilliant-cut diamonds. The emerald cut is the calmest, most mirror-like of all the diamond shapes.

The heart-shape stone. Perhaps the most romantic diamond shape, it takes the symbolic pairing of diamonds and love one step further.

end tapers outward toward the shank of the ring.

For years, choosing an emerald-cut stone was a trade-off between sparkle and style (though some women have chosen emerald-cut stones precisely for their understated sparkle). Those who've preferred brilliance have opted for rounds. But now, thanks to patented cutting techniques, it's possible to have sleek emerald-cut shapes with plenty of brilliance:

The Radiant cut—A rectangular stone with 70 facets and a lively sparkle.

The Starburst—Another trademarked rectangular stone cut for fire and sparkle.

FINDING THE RIGHT SHAPE FOR YOU

Most women fantasize about diamonds in the abstract. Until an engagement is imminent, there's no real reason to try rings on. Consequently, even when a woman is sure she wants an emerald-cut stone, or any other shape for that matter, until she actually spends a few Saturdays trying on rings, there's no way of knowing what looks good on her hand, and what shape or style is most pleasing. Some helpful information:

Much of the plain common sense that goes into an important clothing purchase can be applied to buying an engagement ring. (The biggest difference: the price tag is higher.) You consider the beauty and workmanship of an item, and how it looks on. You factor in your budget and lifestyle, and the quality of what you're buying. If you buy wisely and well, you will wear your purchase for years to come, and the cost-per-wearing amortizes over time.

Clearly, the first factor to consider is how different shape stones look on your hand. Women with short fingers may choose a marquise-shape stone. Tapered to a point on both ends, this shape creates the visual illusion of elongating the finger. Women with very long, thin fingers might find a round stone or a pear shape most pleasing. The rounded edges create a softening effect that makes fingers look less long—the way horizontal stripes flatter a tall, thin body. If an emerald-cut stone is your choice, try long thin rectangles and stones with squarish shapes to see which are most flattering to your fingers and hand.

Can any woman wear any size stone? Just as any woman can wear any style garment as long as the proportion is right for her, the same applies to diamonds. A small woman, for example, can wear a large stone, as long as the setting is very simple, and she has the right attitude. Designer Paloma Picasso, who creates a number of rings in each collection she produces exclusively for Tiffany & Co, is 5'4", and she maintains that "If someone is small, but she has a strong personality and strong features, she can carry off a large ring perfectly." Likewise, a very tall woman can wear a small stone. She may want to choose an elaborate mounting, like a cluster setting or a ring with a heavier band, or she may opt for something perfectly simple and streamlined. In terms of width of a setting, most of the experts say a ring and setting should be no wider than a woman's finger. The stone and baguettes should span from knuckle to knuckle. But this is a matter of comfort. If it's too wide, it will look ungainly and feel uncomfortable.

Basically, it comes down to what you think looks good. You can try on three navy cashmere jackets that vary slightly in style. If you're lucky, one will feel just right. Engagement rings work the same way.

Lifestyle is another factor to consider. Just as a woman who works in advertising wouldn't necessarily wear the same type suit as a woman who works in banking, the same ring isn't right for everyone. One woman whose fiancé surprised her with a gorgeous 3-carat platinum-set stone ten years ago keeps her ring in the safety deposit box because it's out of step with the rest of her life. Now that she is the mother of three and spends the majority of her time driving carpools and taking kids to play dates, the ring is just too large. She only trots it out for special occasions. Another woman, an attorney, bought a half-carat stone that nestles inconspicuously in a plain gold band. Even though she and her husband could afford a larger ring, the understated nature of her stone suits her taste and her life in a conservative, predominantly male law firm. Some lifestyle issues to factor in:

Do you take public transportation to work? If so, you might opt for smaller. (In any event, the New York City Police Department crime prevention unit advises turning your stones to the inside of your hand while you're on the bus or subway.)

Do you work with your hands? Plenty of women— painters, sculptors, gardeners, writers, mothers—feel restrained with any ring on the finger, let alone a large one. These women in particular opt for a single band that serves as a wedding/engagement ring. These rings can be all stones—a so-called Eternity band, or have a few diamonds or other precious stones set at intervals around a gold band.

No, you're not neurotic if you want to go back to a store multiple times before purchasing a ring. Don't be shy about going back as many times as necessary. The stores expect it. At Fortunoff customers come in at least three times. At the Aaron Faber Gallery in Manhattan, couples can look as many as seven or eight times. At Cartier, a customer may come in once and buy, or may come back several times before committing. As much as fancy jewelry stores can be intimidating (the way walking into a Chanel boutique for the first time, or eating in the Time/Warner private corporate dining room for the first time can be unnerving), better jewelers want their customers to take their time, and be certain about their purchase. It's the best guarantee that a customer will be happy with the engagement ring for the duration. And stores look at the purchasing process as the beginning of a beautiful friendship . . . between them and you. They hope to build a relationship, and if the initial experience is satisfying, you'll be back many times in the future for birthday and anniversary gifts.

Popular Ring Styles

For a moment, forget about price and let taste be your guide. Nearly all the ring styles pictured on the next several pages can be created at a variety of price points, depending on the size and quality of the stones (covered in detail in Section II.) Whether hand-crafted at Harry Winston (starting at 2 carats), purchased from the case at Tiffany & Co., bought from a diamond broker in one of America's larger cities, from a jewelry chain at a local mall, or designed by an independent jeweler with an inherited stone—styles found in this section can be had nearly anywhere on practically any budget. This chapter deals specifically with the look of rings—subsequent chapters cover cost, quality, and how to buy.

The Classics

To many, the solitaire, a single round diamond, epitomizes the American engagement ring. Prong-set in platinum or gold, the minimal mounting directs the emphasis to the stone. Though technically termed fancy shapes, rings utilizing a single emerald cut, pear shape, marquise, or oval stone are classics as well. These rings are beautiful in their simplicity—the hallmarks of styles that are here to stay.

A diamond, like a little black dress, is infinitely accessorizable. Pair it with baguettes, tapered or plain. Flank a center stone with trillions, or pear-shape stones. Another classic concept is the three-stone ring. The center stone may be one-third larger than the side stones, or all three stones may be of equivalent shape or size. The side stones may be diamonds, or colored gems like sapphires, emeralds, or rubies. The beauty of a three-stone ring (or even a five-stone ring) is that it creates a big look for less. The price of a ring that has 2 carats of diamonds total weight, spread among three stones, costs less than a 2-carat solitaire. If all three stones are of reasonable quality, they'll wink and catch the light beautifully.

Classic diamonds are elegant alone, or glamorous when accessorized:
From Fortunoff, a prong-set brilliant-cut stone, with 18K yellow gold
mounting, and a beautiful pear-shape stone, also set in 18K gold—
the utmost in simplicity; an oval center stone paired with long, slim
marquise-shape side stones; and a marquise center stone, offset by
trillions, also mounted on 18K gold bands. Notice how the jeweler
has used platinum heads on all these classics so that a white metal is
next to the stone— a visual trick to enhance a diamond's whiteness.

The cool beauty of platinum-set classics: An elegant star-burst-cut diamond, set with trillions; a striking marquise-shape diamond flanked by pear-shape side stones.

A traditional 1-carat round brilliant diamond engagement ring in a platinum setting with tapered baguettes; a romantic, heart-shaped .75-carat diamond solitaire ring, set in 14K gold—completely simple, the curve of the shank echoes the heart-shape stone; a 1-carat oval diamond with channel-set

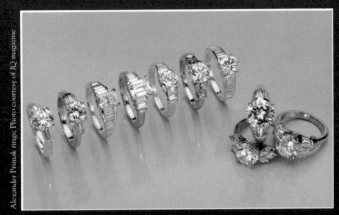

The versatile baguette: Whether a center stone is emerald cut or round, baguettes, set vertically or horizontally, enhance the beauty of the ring, and give it more eye-catching sparkle.

Tiffany & Co. three-stone rings and a classic marquise: A round center stone keeps company with pear-shaped emeralds in this 18K gold-and-platinum-set three-stone ring; a regal marquise set with tapered baguettes in platinum; a three-stone ring, with all emerald-cut stones, of a diamond and two sapphires with an 18K gold band.

Contemporary Looks

Contemporary engagement rings are to jewelry what jazz is to classical music: design with a bit of syncopation, a hip riff on a classic theme. Today it's possible to find rings that are sculptural (John Atencio), architectural (Whitney Boin), or even minimalist to the point that no prongs are needed.

One popular trend is rings that look Etruscan, as if inspired by artifacts from a Fertile Crescent dig. Popularized by goldsmiths Reinstein and Ross, these rings include design details such as braiding and bezel-set stones, in a wonderful range of exotic golds. Imaginative use of metal is taken in another direction by designers who mix different metals for a truly contemporary twist. Platinum and 18-karat gold are swirled together in an unorthodox manner, or golds in unusual hues are intermingled to emphasize geometric designs.

For women who tire of the look of a classically-set diamond, contemporary settings are a popular choice for remounting stones. The following pages reveal a small sampling of the range of imaginative and fascinating ring styles from leading contemporary designers.

Contemporary platinum-set rings with a flowing, sculptural quality by Nova Stylings. Stones are round brilliants and baguettes.

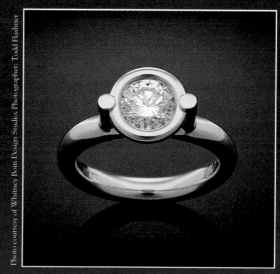

Minimalist and architectural, this Whitney Boin "Post Ring" suspends a stone between two spare columns of 18K gold, instead of traditional prongs.

Photo courtesy of Reinstein and Ross

Reinstein and Ross rings have a modern feel that looks ancient in inspiration, due to design details such as braiding and bezel-set stones. Wonderful golds in chartreuse, peach, and apricot tones intensify the archeological treasure effect. The stones are cabochon and faceted sapphires in every color in the rainbow, a beautiful diamond alternative.

Grandmother's rings never looked like these: Paul Morelli prongsets pear, square, round, or marquise diamonds in an 18K gold collar of metal, with side baguettes. (inset) Tiny spheres add contemporary flair to rings in 18K white or yellow gold, also with baguettes.

A number of designers now mix platinum, or white gold with yellow gold in ring designs, a combination that works well with jewelry or watches that mix stainless steel with yellow metals. Bagley & Hotchkiss, Ltd. has created a beautiful collection of contemporary rings mixing yellow and white gold, yellow, white, and rose gold, and platinum and yellow golds.

Designed and copyrighted by Sam Lehr

The bold new look of rings from Sam Lehr Designs. Round, oval, marquise, and emerald-cut center stones are accented by princess-cut side stones. Because there is no metal between the stones, the mounting creates the illusion of one very large stone. The net effect is pure sparkle!

Diamond Ring Alternatives

The most exciting development in engagement rings today is the broad definition of what an engagement ring can be. It's open to interpretation. In addition to traditional diamond solitaires, couples are choosing colored gems like sapphires, emeralds, or rubies as a center stone, flanked by side diamonds or baguettes. The pearl, widely used in engagement rings in Japan, can be found in suitable mountings here. The beauty of diamond ring alternatives is that you can get more for your money. For $1,500, for example, it's possible to find a larger and better quality sapphire than a diamond for the same price. Part of the appeal of these rings is that they are something different, a reflection of individual taste.

If you do choose a diamond alternative, know that other gems are softer and less durable. Although sapphires are second in hardness to diamonds, emeralds are particularly soft and prone to scratches. Protect softer stones with mountings that cover the girdle—i.e., a bezel setting, or one with side stones like trillions that sit flush against the center stone and minimize its exposure to nicks.

Contemporary designs are redefining what an engagement ring
can be. In addition to traditional diamond solitaires, couples are
choosing colored gems like sapphires, emeralds, or rubies as a center stone, flanked by side diamonds or baguettes. Here, a Gem
Platinum Manufacturing sapphire ring is flanked by triangular-cut

The pearl, widely used in engagement rings in Japan, can be found in mountings suitable for engagement rings here in the United States. A superb example: Barbara Heinrich's 18K and freshwater button pearl ring, with two side diamonds.

A true departure from the past, couples have now begun choosing band rings (also known as guard rings) as engagement rings. The trend has been gaining momentum over the past five years. Also known as Eternity bands, these jeweled hoops might be entirely diamonds, or a mix of diamonds and colored gems, as represented by the breathtaking array of Tiffany & Co. band rings pictured here.

Photo courtesy of *JQ* magazine

Modern, colored gem bands by Alexander Primak. Women wear
jeweled bands in one of three ways: as an engagement ring with a
wedding band; singly as a wedding/engagement ring; or several
stacked (often collected over the years) with a wedding band
mixed in.

Contemporary band rings mixing diamonds and rubies, diamonds and sapphires, or all diamonds. In these rings the 18K band is more substantial and has a presence all its own.

The diamond Eternity band reinterpreted: prong-set round stones alternating with bezel-set baguettes (two baguettes in each bezel create the illusion of a square); bezel-set round diamonds alternating with tapered baguettes; bar-set emerald-cut stones; bar-set baguettes on a slant create a playful zig-zag ring; channel-set princess-cut stones mounted with a mix of platinum and 18K gold.

The Combination Engagement/Wedding Ring

Shortly after Oprah Winfrey announced her engagement to long-time love Stedman Graham, she commented on her television talk show: "I don't like wearing things on my hands, I never have. So I'm not getting an engagement ring in addition to a wedding ring. Just one ring. A *big* one." Like many busy women, a single ring that serves for wedding and engagement best meets her needs. It's a sentiment shared by many active women whose hands are too full, so to speak, to be bogged down with more than one ring. (Admittedly, wearing an engagement ring plus a wedding ring isn't a terribly weighty ordeal. Choosing a single ring is more about psychic ease and simplicity than physical weight.) Many jewelers now offer a variety of mountings, in which the band is up to double the width of traditional engagement rings. All that's missing is the diamond, which you choose.

Photo courtesy of John Atencio

A single ring can have the impact of two with a double-width band.
Or it can be an understated wisp of barely-there diamond baguettes.
John Atencio rings create the appearance of art for the hands—a
single ring is all you need. In "Contours" (left), three terraces of 18K
gold frame the channel-set diamond. The "Prisma Plus" engagement ring (right), features a channel-set Trielle center stone with
princess-cut side stones, also channel-set.

A shimmering take on the Cartier rolling ring: Three bands of gold—rose, yellow, and 18K white—set with pavé diamonds. Originally conceived as a wedding ring, it's also perfect for a combination wedding/engagement ring.

A bit of Byzantium works double-time in this Samuel Jewels wedding/engagement ring. An 18K gold band, 9mm at the widest point, tapering to 6mm in back for comfort, houses a prong-set brilliant-cut stone, and a sprinkling of bezel-set .30 brilliants symmetrically spaced around the band.

WEDDING BANDS

∽

For many couples, selecting wedding bands means the confusion starts all over again. For the bride, the tricky part is finding a band to complement her engagement ring. For the groom, it may be the first time he's ever worn a ring, and the whole issue is bewildering. The mix gets even more complicated when the bride and groom want his-and-her bands that match, not only one another, but the engagement ring as well. Though you'll be plenty preoccupied already, it helps to think about what kind of wedding band you want when selecting an engagement ring. (Traditionally, jewelers discourage this, because research shows that if the rings are purchased separately, the customer will spend significantly more on the engagement ring.) Be an educated shopper. If you can handle thinking about wedding rings without overloading the circuitry, it's wise to begin considering them while looking at engagement rings. Bear in mind that for a woman one way around the question of matching an engagement ring and a wedding ring is to move the engagement ring to the right hand once she is married. By wearing the wedding ring on one hand, and the engagement ring on the other, the metals and styles don't have to match.

What Goes With What?

The most often heard advice is: Choose the same metal for your wedding band that is used on the shank of your engagement ring. Pair platinum with platinum, yellow gold with yellow gold, and so on. It makes good sense, and looks quite seamless and lovely. But plenty of people ignore this advice, for a number of reasons. A woman may have a platinum-set diamond, but she may need a plain gold band for the ceremony (traditional Jewish ceremonies, for example, require a plain gold band). She'll then wear the gold band with her platinum ring. Others simply find the mix of metals pleasing, and choose a gold band with a platinum ring for matters of taste rather than religious conviction. While it's commonplace to see a gold band with a platinum-set engagement ring, it's rare that a woman will choose a platinum wedding band if her engagement ring is set in gold.

Wedding bands to suit every taste at Manhattan's Aaron Faber
Gallery. Top row, left to right: Van Craeynest carved leaf bands in
14K gold with an antiqued finish, for him, and slightly downsized for
her; carved floral motif rings with an antique feel, in 14K gold, for
men and women, also by Van Craeynest. These rings mix particularly well with antique or modern engagement rings. Second row:
Barbara Heinrich's "Milky Way" band in 18K yellow gold with
planets, stars, and diamonds; a 20K gold band embellished with

braiding, and alternating yellow and white diamonds, by J & S English; 20K gold band with two braided rows, also by J & S English; platinum and 18K gold woven together in a classic design, by Nathan Levy. Third row: luxurious bands with an understated feel in 18K gold with decorative platinum patterning, all by Michael Zobel. Bottom: An 18K gold matte-finish band sprinkled with diamonds, by Whitney Boin; a matte platinum Eternity band, also by Boin; a simple 18K gold band.

Beyond the question of metals, anything goes. A woman with a very elaborate engagement ring, or a ring with an exceptional stone may choose a thin, plain band, so as not to detract from her engagement ring. Another woman with a beautiful solitaire may pair it with a simple band that's very wide. Or she may find a jeweled Eternity band most pleasing. And she'll wear both on the same finger. One in five women now buy a diamond wedding band when they get married. Designers are reinterpreting Eternity bands with great creativity. It's now possible to find elaborate bands as well as traditional rings with channel-set baguettes.

Wedding bands, like engagement rings, have come a long way in terms of design. The options span a spectrum from plain metal bands to sculpted pieces of art, as illustrated on the previous two pages. It's now possible to find rings that are quilted or braided. Others have a floral design, the names of couples inscribed *outside*, or a classic millgrain edge (also called beading). Designers like Whitney Boin who specialize in unique engagement rings will design two or three wedding band options that complement the

Whitney Boin 18K yellow gold "Leaf" engagement
ring with matching wedding bands.

diamond mounting. Stores will often display the wedding rings with the engagement rings.

Mixed-metal rings are among the wedding band innovations. Cartier is famous for its Rolling Ring in three golds. Designers like Michael Bondanza, E.B. Harvey, and others have only begun exploring the mix of platinum and 18K gold in wedding rings. The design potential is limited only by their imaginations. Other designers are mixing textures: They'll pair matte or brushed gold with shiny gold to highlight a design, or to be the design itself. And then there are traditional and contemporary wedding bands in unusual golds like apricot or rose.

Mind the Gap?

Another consideration for the bride is the physical fit of the wedding band with the engagement ring. There are two schools of thought. Some believe that the band should sit flush against the engagement ring. For example, if the engagement ring has a marquise shape, the wedding band ought to have a cut-out "V" that nestles against the bottom point of the marquise stone. Jewelers now offer a variety of contour wedding

Photo courtesy of Platinum Guild International U.S.A. Jewelry.

Wedding sets designed to nestle closely. (top) William Schraft
bezel-set engagement rings, with wedding rings contoured to match,
in a mix of platinum and gold. (bottom) A selection of elegantly
classic wedding sets, in platinum, by E.B. Harvey & Company.
Some of the wedding bands pictured mix platinum and 22K gold.

Celebrity Stones

Liz's Latest

"Into every woman's life, a diamond should fall," says Elizabeth Taylor, whose name is synonymous with these precious gems, and whose blockbuster perfume is fittingly called White Diamonds. Over the years, Taylor has been the recipient of many very special diamond pieces, among them the Taylor-Burton, a 69.42-carat pear-shape stone that Taylor sold in 1979, in order to use part of the proceeds to build a hospital in Botswana. Taylor's ring from her new husband Larry Fortensky is 18 karat gold with pavé diamonds.

Eternity

Kelly Klein, wife of designer Calvin, has a ring fit for royalty. Abdicated royalty, that is. Set with glorious emerald-cut diamonds all around, the ring belonged to the Duchess of Windsor, Wallis Simpson. Named "Eternity" by Prince Edward when he presented it to his wife (you know a piece of jewelry is significant when it has a name), the ring provided the inspiration for Calvin Klein's fragrance Eternity.

rings that accommodate all shapes of engagement ring stones, as in the William Schraft and E.B. Harvey wedding sets pictured on page 57. Others believe that it's fine to have a slight gap between the engagement ring and the wedding band. If the center stone is larger than the side stones, the band will sit against the bottom of the diamond, rather than against the shank of the engagement ring, unless the center stone is set particularly high. The majority of rings fit this way. Of course, with bands worn on separate hands, the issue of physical fit is irrelevant.

His and Hers

Some couples choose to match rings for sentimental or symbolic reasons. Others don't. There is no right or wrong. Wedding rings are available in many widths starting at 2mm and going up to 10mm. When couples select the same rings, the groom will often get the band a few millimeters wider than the bride's (6mm is the standard width for men's bands). Some men find a substantial ring more in proportion with the size of their hands. If a man has never worn a ring before, however, he may be most comfortable with a slim band. It may be easier to adjust to the feel of a ring that's smaller and lighter.

Men haven't been excluded from the design innovations now available. Designers like Whitney Boin and Michael Bondanza, who craft wedding rings to go with their engagement rings, also manufacture matching wedding rings in the same designs for men. At the other end of the spectrum are couples who go opposite directions in wedding bands. The bride may choose a platinum band to go with her diamond, but the groom picks a plain gold band.

Plan Ahead
It's wise to plan ahead in selecting and ordering your wedding bands. To be safe, you should order your bands at least two months before the wedding. If your wedding is in June or around Christmas, order even earlier. If the bands have to be custom-made it gives enough time to get the work done. Also, many stores require at least two weeks to a month for engraving.

THE BUYER'S GUIDE

THE STONE

Whether you buy a mounted ring, or you start from scratch and design your own, it's important to have a working knowledge of diamonds. More than 75 percent of engaged couples choose a diamond ring. But diamonds are as complicated as they are beautiful, so you need to understand what you are looking for in a diamond and what you are paying for in a diamond. Perhaps the best confirmation that diamonds exist in a world apart is that they have their own language and alphabet. Here, a basic glossary of diamond terms:

Fire   The rainbow spectrum and intensity
                of colors created by a diamond.

Brilliance The amount of sparkle a diamond has.

Facets   The polished planes on a diamond
                that direct light through the stone.

Girdle   The rim or edge of the stone; the point of the stone with the largest diameter.

Table   The broad top facet—the largest on any stone.

Culet   The tiny bottom facet of a stone.

Crown   The part of the diamond above the girdle.

Pavilion   The part of the diamond below the girdle.

Jeweler's Loupe   The hand-held instrument with a magnification of ten times, used to view diamonds and jewelry. A loupe is particularly useful for checking a diamond's tiny imperfections.

Diamond Boat   Also known as a diamond trough. A very heavy piece of extremely white paper that is folded in a special manner that allows diamonds to sit in a V-shape trough. This is considered the ideal vehicle for viewing a diamond and evaluating its color.

The Four C's

If you've never bought a diamond before, chances are you've never heard of the four C's. Popularized by the Gemological Institute of America (GIA) in 1953, in order to standardize a language of diamonds, the four C's refer to the color, cut, clarity, and carat weight of these precious stones. In each and every diamond, the four C's are the main characteristics that determine the value of the stone. This chapter tours the four C's, presenting both the standard and inside stories. It also addresses the fifth C—cost, and in the process, helps dispel the sixth C (that no one ever talks about)—confusion.

Color

What jewelers will tell you: It's ironic that in Diamondese the ideal color is no color. A colorless diamond causes light to break up into a fiery rainbow spectrum without any outside color to mar the pyrotechnics. Icy diamonds are rare, and therefore of higher value than stones that have an off-white or yellowish tint. Diamonds are measured on a color scale that goes from D to Z. (The diamond alphabet starts with D rather than A, because the GIA wanted to draw a clear distinction between their scale and the alleged AAA diamonds being traded by some shady characters in the industry at the time.) Stones in the D to F range are considered colorless; those G to J are near colorless; stones graded K to M are faint yellow, and so on through the alphabet.

What you should know: With near colorless stones (G to J), the slight off-white quality is only visible through the underside of a stone, and then usually only when the stone is placed in a special folded piece of white paper known as a diamond boat or diamond trough.

From the top, the part of the stone the world will see, even stones in the I range will appear quite white. (Viewed in the diamond boat, the stone will be tinged yellow at the girdle edges.) Although J color stones have a definite yellow or brown tint when viewed unmounted in a diamond boat, in a mounting even they may still look white.

GIA Color Grading Scale

D E F	G H I J	K L M	N O P Q R	S T U V W X Y Z	Fancy Light	Fancy	Fancy Intense
Colorless	Near Colorless	Faint Yellow	Very Light Yellow	Light Yellow	Yellow		

Stones in the Z+ range are called Fancy or colored diamonds. They occur in a range of colors including brown, yellow, blue, and pink and are valuable because of their rare color. Yellow and brown shades are the most plentiful. The most desirable of the stones have a bright brown or yellow tint, rather than a washed-out hue.

This book uses the GIA grading scales for color and clarity. Other grading systems do exist, but the GIA scales are highly recognized and very well known both here and abroad. Most good jewelers will be able to translate their color and clarity scales into GIA terminology.

Cut

What jewelers will tell you: A diamond's cut refers to its overall proportions. This is the only one of the four C's determined by human skill rather than mother nature. (Many first-time buyers confuse cut with diamond shape.) More than any other characteristic, this "C" determines how sparkly and fiery your stone will be. Modern brilliant diamonds are cut with 58 facets—precise planes that direct light in through the top of the stone and out again back toward the eye to create scintillation or sparkle. Certain prominent jewelers claim that "lesser quality" diamonds are "spread"—an extra 10 to 25 percent of the stone is left on to make the stone larger, sacrificing ideal proportions.

What you should know: If you're happy with how much interplay of light there is, the sparkle and fire of the stone, it really doesn't matter if some light is escaping through the pavilion of the diamond rather than being redirected by the cut through the stone's top. While there are textbook ideals for proportions, (the table should be 53 percent of the diameter of the stone, according to the mathematician Tolkowsky) this is only one school of thought. Many in the business believe that "spread" is more a function of taste than of quality cutting. Americans consider anything between 53 to 64 percent normal and reasonable, with preferences running to a wider table (59 to 64 percent.) Parisians prefer even wider tables, up to 66 percent. But the Japanese seem to favor diamonds with a smaller table (58 to 62 percent.) The GIA doesn't consider a 55 percent table any better than 60 percent.

In the industry, diamond dealers refer to cut and proportion as the "make" of a stone. A well-cut stone can cost as much as 50 percent more than a diamond with a poor make. As a rule, stones with small tables have more fire, stones with large tables more brilliance. With cut it's possible to err at both ends of the spectrum. A shallowly-cut stone might look bigger than a well-cut stone of the same carat weight, but the flat stone will appear less sparkly. A stone that is cut too deep will appear smaller than a well-cut stone of the same weight. It may look dark because of the depth, but it may still have plenty of sparkle. Ideally, a diamond balances the two characteristics. Look at individual stones to determine what suits your taste.

Clarity

What jewelers will tell you: This "C" refers to the number of imperfections visible inside the stone. Truly flawless stones are exceedingly rare. Most, when magnified at a high enough power, reveal some flaws. In principal, the more flawless the stone, the more readily light passes through the diamond because a diamond with high clarity has fewer inclusions that obstruct the flow of light. Clarity (determined by a trained eye under ten-power magnification) is graded on a scale of Flawless, Internally Flawless (IF), Very Very Slight Inclusion (VVS1 and VVS2), Very Slight Inclusion (VS1 and VS2), Slight Inclusion (SI1), and so on. The size, location, and quantity of blemishes factor into the clarity. For a complete description, see the chart on the following pages.

Clarity Chart

Flawless (FL)
Exactly what it says. No flaws apparent at ten-power magnification.

IF
Internally flawless. May have slight external scratches or nicks, or minor problems with polishing. Can usually be polished out. As with flawless stones, IF stones are exceedingly rare and valuable, all other C's being equal.

VVS1
Very very slight pinpoint inclusions and/or external blemishes at or near the edge. These flaws are very difficult to locate under ten-power magnification.

VVS2
Very very slight inclusions generally under the table of the stone. Very difficult to locate under ten-power magnification.

VS1
Very slight inclusions generally near the edge of the stone. Difficult to locate under ten-power magnification.

VS2   Very slight blemishes near in the heart of the stone. Difficult to locate under ten-power magnification.

SI1   Slightly included; blemishes toward the edge of the stone that are fairly easy to locate under ten-power magnification.

SI2   Slightly included; flaws are under the table of the stone and fairly easy to locate with ten-power magnification.

I1   Included; blemishes are very easy to locate under ten-power magnification.

I2   Heavily included; blemishes in the heart of the stone that are very easy to locate with the naked eye.

I3   Extremely heavy inclusions easily located with the naked eye.

What you should know: Some jewelers refer to the flaws of a diamond as the "fingerprint" of the stone. Each one is unique, each has its little hiccups. But in stones graded SI2 clarity and above, most flaws listed below are not visible to the untrained naked eye and can be seen only with a jeweler's loupe (magnification of ten). So unless you run with a crowd that makes a habit of carrying jeweler's loupes . . . you're set. (The exception is emerald-cut stones. The faceting arrangement on these rectangular stones acts like a window into the stones and flaws in even SI2 clarity diamonds are visible. With an emerald cut, it's best to stay with SI1 or above, if you want your ring to look "eye-clean.") Flaws also called inclusions or identifying characteristics include:

Crystals—Also called diamonds within diamonds, these crystals (which can sometimes be of other minerals) literally grow against the grain of the rest of the diamond.

Pinpoint inclusions—Also mistakenly called carbon spots, are tiny specks of crystal or thin flat blemishes that reflect light like a mirror and in so doing make the spot look black.

Clouds—Clusters of miniscule crystals that give an area a hazy or cloudy appearance.

Feathers—A central crack, with little cracks radiating from it at times.

Chips—A nick (external) in the girdle of the stone.

Scratch—A surface flaw that can usually be polished out.

All flaws decrease the value of a diamond. Colorless flaws such as crystals are preferred to black flaws that darken the stone. A flaw at the edge of the stone is preferable to one at the center, where it intercepts the primary path of light, and if big enough, is visible through the table. A good jeweler may be able to mount a diamond in such a way that a prong or setting masks a side flaw. Flaws buried deep within a diamond are preferable to those touching the top or side surface. A feathery crack near the surface can actually expand if the diamond suffers an impact.

Also, many jewelers are of the opinion that flawless diamonds belong in a bank vault. Once mounted, even the most flawless stone can develop nicks or scratches through ordinary wear and tear.

Rings Around the Country

The 1992–93 Jeweler's Almanac, a yearly publication by JCK (Jeweler's Circular-Keystone, a trade publication for the jewelry industry) lists median ranges of the 4 C's for engagement rings sold in 1990: Cost: $2,200; Color: H; Carat Weight: 60 pt.; Clarity SI1. We did a bit of informal polling/trend reporting at stores around the country, and here are the results:

• At Fortunoff, a large jeweler based in Westbury, New York, the H SI range is the average quality sold. In terms of shapes, rounds are first, pear second, and marquise a very close third. Most people buying a ring come in at least twice, and typically have shopped three other stores before purchasing at Fortunoff.

• At Shreve, Crump & Lowe, Boston, Massachusetts, the average range for engagement rings is G VS (H SI1 is the lowest quality they sell). The average size for solitaires is 1 carat to 1.25. Three-stone diamond and sapphire rings are big sellers, and always have been, with either the diamond or sapphire used as a center stone. Lately, this Boston store has been selling a number of jeweled bands as engagement rings. Another growing trend is five-stone bands with a total weight of 1.3 to 1.75 carats in diamonds.

•At Tivol, in Kansas City, Missouri, the average size diamond sold is ¾-carat. The average color is above GH. The average clarity is VS2 to SI1. Their mountings are almost entirely 18K gold, but all the bigger rings are done in platinum. Tivol provides a GIA certificate with every center stone they sell. Fifty percent of rings sold are already mounted, 50 percent start with loose stones.

•At Borsheim's in Omaha, Nebraska, engagement rings with ½-carat to 1 carat are the most popular sizes. G to J is the most popular color range. The average clarity is SI to VS. Although Borsheim's does sell some mounted rings, most engagement rings are semi-mounts—the mountings have baguettes or side stones, but are waiting for the couple to choose a loose center stone.

• Mayor's, in Ft. Lauderdale, Florida, in the Galleria Mall, reports that while round stones are still number one, and marquises are quite popular, they've been selling a surprising number of oval stones. More than ever before couples are choosing rings that incorporate channel-set baguettes on either side of the center stones. In general, Mayor's sells diamonds that are SI clarity or better and HI or better color. Although 90 percent of the rings they sell are already mounted, Mayor's has a full-time designer who does custom rings.

• At Richard D. Eiseman, in Dallas, Texas, some 60 percent of engaged couples are choosing to incorporate colored gemstones into their engagement rings, instead of traditional solitaires. A newer but growing trend is the use of colored stones as a center stone flanked by diamonds. The majority of ring buyers who go for diamond and colored stone mixes are opting for a single ring with a more substantial band that serves as a wedding/engagement ring. At this Texas store, the most popular diamond grades are G to H color, with VS2 to SI clarity.

•At Altobelli Jewelers, in North Hollywood, California, more than 20 percent of their customers utilize the firm's forty-four-year-old design studio to create unusual custom pieces. The store makes up most of its own mountings, but they do carry some pieces from other designers. These days, engaged couples are buying larger diamonds, many over 1-carat. Although the stones are eye-clean, usually VS1 to SI1, the colors typically fall in the J to K range.

Carat

What jewelers will tell you: A carat is the measure of diamond weight. The term actually comes from ancient India where gems were measured against the weight of carob seeds, a measure that eventually became standardized. (A carat equals one-fifth of a gram.) One carat is divided into 100 "points." The higher the carat weight, the larger the stone. Most jewelers will tell you that it's impossible to assess the value of a diamond from its carat weight alone. Says one jeweler: That's like saying how much is a car that has four wheels? But when cut, clarity, and color are all good, the larger the diamond, the more expensive it will be. With truly fine stones, the price difference between 1 and 2 carats can vary by thousands of dollars.

What you should know: In America, we're conditioned to THINK BIG. Jewelers will gladly encourage customers to buy large, good quality stones, because they make more money on the deal. In fact, a fine quality 2-carat brilliant stone costs more than two times a 1-carat brilliant stone of the same quality, because larger stones are rarer, and therefore more valuable. However, when polled privately, most jewelers agree that carat size is the least important of the 4 C's. Women who sacrifice quality to buy a large stone are the first to grow tired of their rings. Conversely, couples who choose a small stone with terrific color, fire, and brilliance are happy with their purchase for years.

Prioritizing the 4 Cs

Unless your budget is unlimited, buying a diamond is a series of compromises and trade-offs as you find a pleasing balance of color, clarity, cut, and size. Which C is the most negotiable? Here are the trade-offs you might consider, as recommended by a number of jewelers:

Carat weight first: Go smaller. If a stone is small but pretty, it will be pleasing to the wearer for many years.

Clarity second: To the naked eye, a D Flawless diamond and a D SI1 stone look identical. By trading down in clarity the price differences can be in the tens of thousands.

Color third: A 1-carat D VS2 stone and a G VS2 of comparable cut look the same to the untrained eye. But the G color stone costs thousands less. It's possible to trade down—as far down as an H to J color and still have a diamond that looks quite white and pretty when mounted. And the savings are significant.

Cut last: Although a D Flawless stone that has a poor cut costs as much as 50 percent less than a comparable stone that's beautifully cut, it will have less liveliness and sparkle than a diamond that's near white in color and in the SI range in clarity.

How to Look at
a Diamond

It's one thing to look for a diamond. It's another mat-ter entirely to look at a diamond properly. Factors as diverse as the lighting conditions and the piece of paper on which you view a stone can affect whether you see the stone properly. Let's start with:

Jewelry Store Lighting

In Hollywood, the hour before sunset is referred to as the Magic Hour. It's the cinematographer's choice for shooting romance scenes. The sun, round and orange on the horizon, bathes everything in the most gorgeous, glowing light.

At jewelry stores, every hour is Magic Hour. Jewelry store lighting is designed to transform diamonds into dancing prisms of light. Most stores from the highest end to the lowest rent have spotlights fitted with incandescent bulbs trained right on the diamond case. These lights have a high amount of the red spectrum, which makes even a yellow diamond seem sparkling and scintillating.

The problem is, once you bring the stones home, or out in the sunlight, potentially you're in for a letdown. (Any woman who has ever purchased foundation or lipstick at a department store will recognize this phenomenon.)

It's something of a double standard. No jeweler would ever purchase a diamond that he'd only viewed under a spotlight. To the naked eye, the first seven diamond color grades are difficult to distinguish—even for the experts. If you view a diamond in this color range under spotlights, the differences are even further muted.

For years, northern daylight was considered the best, most consistent lighting in which to grade diamonds. Every diamond firm in the world had a picture window facing north. These days, diamond dealers have daylight fluorescent bulbs that simulate the best light when they look at stones. Although most stores are outfitted with spotlights, they generally have windows to the outside world. "It's best to look at stones in north daylight or indirect sunlight. If need be, bring the diamond right to the edge of the door," advises Roy Albers, chief gemologist at Tiffany & Co.

But you need to be concerned with more than just lighting. Ted Mandell and his partner Howard Schwartz run a Manhattan-based jewelry firm and diamond brokerage called the Diamond Vault. They also teach a course called "Don't Get Taken When Buying a Diamond, or What Jewelers Would Rather You Never Know" at New York City's Discovery Center. Mandell, a self-styled advocate for diamond-buying couples, speaks plainly about the diamond-buying process. "You have to be as cautious as if you were buying an automobile. A used one." According to Mandell, the only way to look at diamonds is unmounted (mountings can hide flaws), face down, in a diamond boat under the proper lighting. Other experts in the business agree, and add that couples should look at stones side-by-side, viewing one loose stone, putting it away, and then viewing another loose stone. Having the benefit of comparison is tremendously important in determining what best suits a given couple. "If you're not willing to go to this trouble (and since many retail jewelers are not set up for customers to look at stones this way), then you have to have a hired gun. In this case," says Mandell, "it's the GIA."

For added assurance that what you are buying is actually what you are getting, make your purchase contingent upon a GIA certificate. The GIA, known in the industry as the Harvard of gemology, popularized the four C's and standardized much of the diamond terminology in current use. With branches in New York and Santa Monica, and satellite offices in Tokyo and London, the GIA is internationally recognized as the final arbiter in diamond grading and verification. For each diamond that comes into the GIA testing labs in New York and California, as many as six experts grade it, giving exact measurements, weight, color grading, clarity, and proportions. They do not, however, assign a monetary value—they will only specify the exact characteristics of the diamond.

As a wholly independent body that does not sell stones or jewelry, the GIA certificate is the preferred certificate among diamond dealers and manufacturers in New York. Most agree that any stone that's 1 carat or larger, and G VS2 or better, ought to come with a certificate verifying this. Although some stores, such as Tivol in Kansas City, include a certificate with each stone they sell, often it's necessary to request certification. Generally, a jeweler will pass along the cost to the customer. The cost is based on the weight of the stone—to grade a 1 to 1.49 carat diamond costs approximately $120, and the GIA will only grade loose stones.

Independent laboratory grading takes the guesswork out of buying a diamond. Most jewelers have nothing to hide, and they'll be happy to make the sale contingent upon GIA verification. Out-of-town jewelers routinely send stones overnight to New York for this purpose. If you find that your jeweler is resistant to doing this, you may want to rethink your choice of jeweler.

For stones that are already mounted, jewelers can either remove the stone for testing, or they can send the ring to the next preferred independent testing lab—the International Gemological Institute (IGI), also in New York, where loose or mounted stones can be graded from $95 for 1 to 2 carat stones. IGI provides a monetary value as part of their grading certificate.

A Note on Fluorescence

Roughly 50 percent of all diamonds have some degree of fluorescence. (Unless a stone is accompanied by a certificate, most couples never hear this term.) Fluorescence is a natural effect. When the crystal matrix of diamonds is forming, certain gas atoms can be trapped. When exposed to UV rays, those atoms get excited, and vibrate until they light up like neon. Under a black light (UV) diamonds fluoresce blue, chalky white, whitish yellow, yellow, and orange. Or not at all.

Fluorescence is a case in which a little bit can't hurt, and might even help. So if your diamond report reads Fluorescence: None to Medium, don't panic. Slightly yellow stones in the J to M color range that have a medium fluorescence often appear brighter in daylight (sunlight has UV rays—that's why we use sunblock!). However, when stones have a high degree of fluorescence, it cuts down on the value. Highly fluorescent diamonds look oily or milky in sunlight. And even when facets are well cut, the fluorescence makes them seem less sharp.

If You Are a Man, Read This

The best piece of advice my husband has to offer after shopping with me for a ring is: Men, if you're not sure what shape and style ring your fiancée wants, ASK. It's unlikely she'll steer you wrong.

If you do go for the surprise, make certain that the ring is exchangeable. Be sure the exchange/return policy is stated on the bill of sale.

The safest route is shopping for the ring together (more than 70 percent of engaged couples do). You can even shop together and still surprise her: Choose a stone together, and have your fiancée pick out three mountings she really likes. You make the final choice and the ring is still a surprise.

If your eyes glaze over when talk turns to ring styles, you're not alone. According to jewelers, men are more interested in the quality of the stone. Women are more interested in the total look of the ring.

If you get burned out shopping, take a breather. Let your fiancée spend a day trying on rings on her own. When she has a clearer idea of what she wants, then you can help choose the final style.

GETTING SET
Metals and Mounting

Once you've determined what diamond shape
most appeals to you, it's time to consider the
mounting. It's important to choose a mounting that
reflects your personal style. A ring can be simple and
classic. Modern and architectural. Ornate. Sporty.
Yellow gold or platinum. Realize that the mounting
you choose dramatically affects the look of a stone on
your hand.

If ever there's a gender gap in ring buying, here it
is. Most jewelers note that while men are very concerned about the specifics of the quality of the stone,
women are more concerned about the mounting and
the net effect the ring will have on her hand.

A Test of Metal
The first thing to consider is the metal, and you will
be faced with two choices: the color of the metal (yel-

A traditional marquise: Prong-set in platinum, with tapered baguettes, this Tiffany & Co. marquise engagement ring has a very clean classic look.

Turned on its side and bezel-set in 18K gold, with princess-cut accent stones, this Sam Lehr marquise ring has a wonderfully modern look.

low or silver/white are the traditional options) and the actual type of metal (platinum versus white or yellow gold, and if you choose gold, 18 karat or 14 karat).

A "karat" is a measure of gold purity. (Not to be confused with a "carat," which is a measure of gemstone weight.) Pure gold contains 24 parts pure gold (24K) and no alloys. Eighteen karat gold (18K) contains 18 parts pure gold and 6 parts alloy. Fourteen karat gold has a ratio of 14 parts pure gold to 10 parts alloy. Many jewelers in Europe and some in the states stamp 18K gold as .750 because it is 75 percent pure. Likewise 14K gold will be marked .585.

Let's address the color issue first: Conventional jewelry wisdom dictates that if your stone is a very fine white color (D, E, or F), you should set it in platinum (or white gold, if you're on a budget) because yellow gold can actually throw yellow color onto the stone and make it look less white. And if your stone is slightly yellow in color, setting it in yellow gold can make the diamond look whiter by contrast. Yet not all jewelers agree. The Cartier Engagement Ring, for example, is a diamond mounted on a band of three colors of 18K gold—yellow, white, and rose. (Cartier

The Cartier Engagement Ring, available in round, marquise, emerald, pear, oval, or starburst, mounts a diamond on three merging bands of rose, yellow, and white 18K gold.

only uses stones with grades of D to H, FL to VS2.) Says Brian Lange, assistant vice president of marketing for Cartier, "If your stone is in the JKL range and set in yellow gold it tends to bring out the yellow in the stone. But if you have a stone that is DEF, VS2 clarity or above, it looks pretty darn good in yellow gold. It depends on the look you want."

The Type of Metal

Color aside, the other questions to consider when choosing the metal in your mounting are strength of metal, how it wears, and your budget. There's no question that platinum is both more durable and more expensive. Platinum is considered a noble metal—one that is pure. Unlike gold, it isn't measured in karats. Most platinum rings are stamped PT 950, meaning 95 percent platinum. The other 5 percent is usually ruthenium, another metal in the platinum family. If money is no object, and a white metal is your preference, you should choose platinum. But be sure that jewelers in your area are equipped to handle the upkeep. Not all jewelers are experienced in working with platinum. Some jewelers "fudge" and repair platinum with gold—a maneuver that's sloppy and unacceptable.

And if neither white nor yellow metal works for you, gold is available
in a rainbow of colors—red, green, pink—all created by variations
in the alloy. (The addition of copper produces reddish-pink tints;
fine silver creates greenish casts.) At Reinstein and Ross, goldsmiths
in New York City who produce a number of engagement rings, clients
can have stones set in 18K chartreuse gold, 20K peach gold, or 22K
apricot gold, as pictured here.

A contemporary setting that skirts the prong issue entirely: The Steven Kretchmer "Tension Set" ring suspends a diamond in midair, without prongs. This effect is made possible by the unique strength of platinum.

If, however, your tastes run to gold, don't be overly concerned with the difference in strength. "Yes, platinum is stronger," says Lange, "but 18K gold is strong enough that it doesn't present a problem." With gold, you have a choice of 18 karat or 14 karat. If you're looking to save money on the setting, know that 14K has a lower gold content and is therefore less expensive. The advantage of 14K gold rings is that they tend to be sturdy and strong; a disadvantage is that over a period of many years, the gold can discolor due to the high content of alloy metals like copper. But the situation is reversible. "Just as shoes that are badly scuffed can be restored by a professional shine, a ring repolished by a competent jeweler can be restored to a nice gold color," says Mark Mann, deputy manager, on-campus education for GIA, in Santa Monica.

Eighteen karat gold has a higher gold content, but it is also softer. It's not uncommon to see 18K gold estate rings on which the back of the band is worn very thin—the gold actually wears away. "If you're choosing between 14K and 18K gold mountings of similar styles, a well-made 18K piece should be a little thicker, because the engineering of the 18K piece is slightly different to compensate for the metal's more malleable quality," explains Mann.

If you know you want the look of a white metal around your stone but are concerned about cost, white gold is an option to consider. The color of white golds, both 14K and 18K, is only slightly less white than platinum. And both golds are routinely plated in rhodium, a metal in the platinum family, to turn the color a pure white. White gold, particularly 18K, has something of a reputation for being too brittle to hold diamonds. In reality, the biggest downside to white gold is for the jeweler rather than the consumer. White gold alloys contain a lot of nickel—which is less malleable than gold or platinum and more difficult for jewelers to work with. But once a stone is set well, many jewelers believe that the brittleness is not that significant. The white gold mounting is still harder than a yellow gold metal of the same karatage.

You Can Have It Both Ways

Finally, if you prefer a yellow gold band, but don't want to detract from the whiteness of the stone, the jeweler can make the prongs surrounding the center diamond in a white metal. Many jewelers set solitaire diamonds in platinum (or white gold) whether the shank of the band is 18K gold or platinum. When a center diamond of a three-stone ring is flanked by rubies, sapphires, and emeralds, the center is set in platinum while the colored stones are held by gold prongs.

Metal Sensitivities

One out of every eleven people is allergic to nickel, a common alloy metal in white gold, and less frequently in yellow gold. Nickel is the most common cause of allergic dermatitis. According to Dr. Alexander Fisher, clinical professor of dermatology at New York University Medical Center, the signs of a nickel allergy are red and itchy skin under the ring, and little bumps and blisters when you remove the ring. With application of cortisone cream the rash will go away shortly. The more permanent solution is a new mounting made of platinum, or of gold without nickel in the alloy. Gold rarely causes allergies. And when it does, the rash is thicker and more persistent. By contrast to nickel and gold, platinum is hypoallergenic.

A Setting Primer

There's a logic to the way a jeweler sets stones in each and every ring. The manner in which a stone is set has as much to do with keeping it securely in the ring as with the design aesthetics. Here, a round-up of some basic setting styles and terminology.

Prong set: Far and away the most popular for engagement rings are little fingers of metal that clasp the girdle of the stone. Four- and six-prong styles are used with the basic stone shapes, and ideally, prongs have a smooth ball head that sit flush with the stone. V-shape prongs can be used to hold the points of marquise and pear-shape stones for added security. Out of all the mountings, the prong leaves the most stone exposed. This can be a positive and a negative: On the plus side, it exposes the stone to the most light and shows it off to best advantage. On the negative, there is more girdle exposed to potential damage and nicks.

Bead set/pavé: Pavé literally means paved with diamonds. Holes are drilled into a sheet of metal in which stones will sit. The metal that is displaced by the drilling is raised into a bead and some of that metal is pushed around each stone to hold it in place. Although the stones are well protected while they are in the setting, pavé stones can fall out. And since the stones are usually small, you don't see them fall. So fixing a pavé ring often means replacing lost stones.

Bezel set: A collar of metal is fitted around the entire girdle of the stone. In terms of technique, it is basically the same as channel set, but for the individual stone. A variation, a half-bezel setting, can be used with three-stone rings to create the appearance that all three stones are really one larger stone. A single rim of metal surrounds the outside of the three stones. The side stones sit flush against the center stone with no metal in between. This is a very secure setting as all of the girdle is protected by the bezel. Bezel settings are a great option for old stones that are worn at the edges. On the downside, a gold bezel can make a white stone look slightly yellower than it is because so much gold metal encloses the stone.

Channel set: Frequently used in Eternity bands, two rims of metal (like curbs at either side of a street, or two banks at opposite sides of a river) hold the stones in place. No metal is between the stone, just at the outer edges, like a retaining wall. An advantage to channel-set bands is that the stones are very well protected and unlikely to loosen up. But every jeweler has stories of women breaking stones in Eternity bands, especially the stones underneath the finger. Baguettes are more prone to breakage than round stones in a channel setting. Quite simply, they are longer and thinner and that makes them more vulnerable.

Bar setting: Vertical bars of metal between stones hold them in place. These settings are very attractive because the bars are very thin, and a lot of stone is exposed. But for the same reason bar-set rings won't tolerate much of a beating. The edges are exposed, so there is leverage on the stones, and they can easily loosen up.

MOUNTING EVIDENCE
Engagement Ring Trends

For many years, women favored solitaires set in a high mounting. The reason being, the higher the stone off the hand, the more light would pass through it, and the more sparkly it would be. Or so they thought. In reality, a well-cut stone will be sparkly whether set high or low, in a bezel setting or a traditional six-prong Tiffany setting. (Settings that have a lot of metal around the stone may darken the stone a bit, but the stone will still sparkle if it is cut well.)

Today, there is a trend toward lower settings. Rings set high have a greater chance of catching prongs on hair, clothing, even dishtowels, in the course of daily activity. Lower mountings (including antique and period rings which tend to have settings low to the hand) are less precarious and better protect stones, making them well suited to women's active lifestyles.

As prong-set engagement rings are the most popular

in this country, it's no surprise that the greatest number of repairs on engagement rings are on prongs. Paul Phelps, a jeweler at Osborn-Phelps in Manhattan, who sees rings with broken prongs come through his workshop on a regular basis, explains that in making prongs, many things can go wrong: The jeweler can make the notch in which the stone fits too deep, so the prong is weak from the start. If the prongs aren't smoothed and finished nicely they will catch easily, and can break or pull away from the stone. Or, in the final stages, the polisher can shear away too much metal, making the prong too thin. When buying a ring, check the prongs by:

• Holding the ring to your ear and gently shaking. If the stone is loose (an indication that something is amiss with the prongs) you'll hear a delicate clinking sound.

• Check that the prongs have a smooth bead or ball at the end, and that the bead is pressed tightly to the stone. If the head of the prong is not pressed tightly over the stone just above the girdle, then it can catch on threads, stockings, or hair. (Avoid prongs that are clipped off straight. It's a cheap, time-saving method for making prongs, but the stone is less securely held.)

• With your pinkie fingernail, gently wiggle the stone between the prongs. If it moves, the prongs need attention.

These tips also apply for checking the security of your stone in between professional check-ups. Most jewelers recommend bringing your ring in every twelve to eighteen months to check the setting. At the same time, they'll give your stone(s) a good, thorough cleaning.

As security is always a concern, know that diamonds with a round shape are the least likely to fall out of their mounting. According to Phelps, if a round stone becomes loosened, it will most likely turn in its bearing. It should be fixed without waiting too long, but you don't have to run to the nearest jeweler. When an oval, marquise, or emerald twists between its prongs, it becomes unsupported and is more likely to fall out. If one of these stones becomes loosened, by all means get it taken care of right away.

You may also want to check the quality of your mounting. Rings can be cast from a mold in a one-shot process, entirely handmade, die-struck (punched out by machine), or any of an infinite combination of partially cast and partially handmade components. Any mountings that are created and finished with care can last for many years and look beautiful. Regardless of the process used to create your mounting, always check to see that:

- The underside of the ring is as clean and beautiful as the topside.

- There are no rough pieces of metal that catch on clothes or bite into fingers.

- The mounting is symmetrical.

- There are no visible blobs of solder.

Finding a Jeweler and Designing Your Own Ring

If you've inherited a stone and want to create an unusual mounting, or if you want to create a ring yourself, and you can't seem to find a ready-made mounting for it in a store, you may need to find a jewelry store with its own design studio, or a jeweler that contracts work out. Finding the right jeweler is like finding a plastic surgeon: Talk to people you know and trust for referrals. If you see work you like, ask where it was done.

Once you're in a jeweler's workshop there are two main issues at hand: One is design competence, the other is workmanship.

Vis à vis design: Most jewelers will have pictures in a portfolio to help you see the range of styles they create. The point of looking is to be certain that the designer has a sensibility that's compatible with your own.

Vis à vis workmanship: Most jewelers will also have trays of sample pieces to show you. Look at the rings carefully.

- If you turn a ring over, the back side should look neat and clean.

- There shouldn't be an excess of solder.

- A ring shouldn't feel very heavy for what it is. You don't want to pay for gold you don't need. The workmanship should be fine, not extra heavy.

- A ring should be polished inside and out.

- Look to see that pieces aren't cracked or filled with bubbles or bumps. A poor jeweler will let simple problems go.

- If you're looking for a platinum ring, check that platinum samples don't show gold solder—a sign of inexperience or incompetence.

- It may be possible to design a ring at your local jewelry shop. If your jeweler can't do the work himself, he may have resources that enable him to contract out the work.

THE PURCHASE
The Fifth C: Cost

Imagine looking at new homes, and asking the real estate broker what you ought to spend. Unheard of, right? No one in his reasonable mind would leave so personal a decision to a perfect stranger. Yet similar situations occur daily in jewelry stores across the country. Engagement rings are the only major purchase for which consumers ask the seller how much they should be spending.

Understandably, couples seek guidance in making a significant purchase like a ring. But while they might be looking for a hard-and-fast rule on what to spend, there just isn't one. The numbers are as rubbery as the fluctuations of the economy. For example, in the free-spending eighties diamond vendors were recommending as much as three months of the man's yearly income as the appropriate sum. (They neglected to specify whether that was before or after taxes!) Today that position has softened to two months' salary. More conservative stores or those located in economically depressed areas advise spending three weeks, or 6 percent of the man's yearly income. The rationale behind all these figures is that couples should spend enough money to purchase a quality ring.

A merchant in one of New York's poshest jewelry boutiques explains it this way: "It's important long-term to buy the best you can. Especially with something that has intrinsic value like diamonds and precious metal. Even in the last couple years, with the economy the way it's been, people want a significant, important ring. The diamond industry has been important in promoting the idea of two months' salary for an engagement ring. It seems like a lot of money. When you think about what you make and multiply it by two and say this is what I'm going to spend on a ring—Wow! That seems like a lot of money. But when you think about the fact that this ring will be worn every day for hopefully thirty, forty, fifty years, it really does make sense to buy something beautiful that will be beautiful to you for a long time. Not something that's going to be great for now. In the event you have children someday, this is even more important. The ring is something you may hand down to a daughter or a daughter-in-law. It's wise to buy better quality in the beginning. It will be in the clients' best interest in the end."

Keeping that advice in mind, what you spend is nobody's business but your own. You need to work out as a couple an appropriate sum (the first of many financial decisions in your life ahead). Set a budget *before* you go shopping. That way you know you'll be looking at rings within your price range. While some couples will push their credit card limit to buy a ring, others don't believe in going into debt. It's important to remember that a diamond ring (or any engagement ring for that matter) is a symbol. If a couple spends less than the recommended two months' salary, does that mean their love is any less than the couple who spends five times that amount?

You also need to bear in mind that while diamonds are forever, their prices are not. Diamonds are a commodity, and the market is subject to extreme fluctuations. In 1979, when times were flush, a 1-carat D Flawless stone went for $62,000. At the time of this writing, the asking price for the same stone among dealers in New York is $15,900. The cost of stones fluctuates with the economy and with supply in the diamond market. Some other rough prices to go by: A 1-carat G VS2 is listing for $4,900, and a 1-carat H SI1 is fetching $4,400.

There are guides in which one can research approximate diamond asking prices. The best known is the Rapaport Diamond Report, a weekly price list published at 15 W. 47 St., New York, NY 10036; (212) 354-0575. But bear in mind, these are asking prices among dealers in New York City. At a diamond brokerage/boutique like New York's Diamond Vault, a stone would go for anywhere from the Rapaport list price to 25 percent below that figure. At an off-price store that does a volume business, diamonds would go for 40 to 50 percent more than the list price. And at name-brand boutiques, the stones would go for significantly more than that. Don't hesitate to do your own market research. For the most accurate sense of diamond pricing in your area, check at least three local stores and/or diamond brokers for the cost of equivalent stones. (The absolute best way to verify that stones are equivalent is to make sure you compare only stones with GIA certificates.) It pays to shop around.

Love and Money

"The Two Months' Salary Guideline can be the most useful tool you have for getting your customers to spend more for their purchase," says a widely-disseminated diamond industry pamphlet on selling higher-priced diamond engagement rings. Many jewelers selling engagement rings rely on the romance of the situation to increase their profits. By playing up the emotional nature of the purchase ("a diamond engagement ring is the purchase of a lifetime, a symbol of love" says the same pamphlet) they hope to sell you, the consumer, on the two-months' salary guideline, and on bigger-ticket items. In addition to this strategy, another selling technique used to get you to spend more is showing customers larger diamonds than they can afford. The alleged rationale is, this tells customers the jeweler thinks they can afford pricier stones, and they want the best the store has to offer. In reality, they are hoping couples will be swept away by the emotion of the situation. And riding the crest of "nothing's too good for the woman you love" you'll drop significantly more cash. Caveat emptor.

A BIG DIAMOND LOOK WITHOUT THE BIG DIAMOND PRICE

More often than not, when a couple asks for budget advice, what they're really asking is, "Can We Get A Beautiful Ring Within Our Price Range?" The answer is yes. Emphatically. There is a perfect stone for every person and every price point. And most jewelers who care about their customer's satisfaction are willing to help. For example, Tiffany & Co., who previously offered engagement rings starting at $4,500, began running ads in 1992 for diamond engagement rings starting at $850. ("For less than you may have believed, a Tiffany diamond is more than you ever imagined.") Consequently, their sales in engagement rings for that year rose 40 percent. While you won't get a 1-carat stone at that price (Tiffany won't compromise their D to I, IF to VS2 standards, so you'll probably get a ring with a one-quarter-carat stone) it will still be a beautiful, precious engagement ring.

The following provides some other strategies from noted experts in the field, including Esther Fortunoff, on getting a big look for less. Fortunoff is executive vice president for the family stores of the same name. She oversees all diamond buying for all five of the New York and New Jersey stores. And what ring does she wear? A 2.5-carat oval. She recommends ovals because they are the least expensive shape. For the same dollars, you can get a bigger oval stone than a round, pear-shape, or marquise. Other ideas include:

A three-stone ring.
If you can't afford a larger stone, a setting with side diamonds makes the center stone look bigger. The total look is more important in terms of size, but you don't have to sink as much into a center stone. The side stones can be very large. One carat in total weight is more value for the money than a 1-carat solitaire.

A five-stone ring.
For approximately $2,000, a five-stone band gives a big diamond look without having a major center stone.

A stylish diamond alternative.

In Japan, pearl engagement rings are big sellers. In Boston, sapphires have always done well. Within the last five years, women have begun choosing band/guard rings as engagement rings. An engagement ring is a personal statement. And these alternatives are often less costly than a traditional diamond solitaire.

The efficient shapes.

Almost any other shaped stone will tend to look bigger than the most popular round shape. It's an optical illusion: Oval, pear, marquise, and emerald-shape stones are more elongated than round stones and therefore look bigger—and they cost less per carat.

Just a *little* smaller.

A full carat marks a significant price step. A .90-carat stone will look essentially the same as a 1-carat stone when mounted, but can cost at least 15 percent less per carat. For example, at the time of this writing, .90 point G SI is listed at $3,900/carat, or $3,510. A 1-carat G SI stone is listed at $4,600. For two stones that will look nearly the same, that's a $1,090 price difference.

Buy small, trade up.
Many stores and dealers have a standing trade-in policy. At Fortunoff, for example, you can always receive the original purchase price of your stone as a credit toward something larger or of greater value—no matter what happens to the price of diamonds. Research the store's policy before you buy.

Spend on the stone, not the trimmings.
Put all your money into the stone, but choose a die-struck 14K gold mounting without baguettes or side-stones. These machine-made mountings can be had for as little as $100 and are sufficiently strong to hold a precious stone. When you can afford to, upgrade to 18K gold or platinum with baguettes.

Timing
The best time to get a good price on a diamond is in January. Throughout November and December diamond prices creep upward. After the holiday rush is over, the prices usually settle back down again. If you can wait until January it will be worth it. July is another month when the jewelry business is slow, and diamond prices are slightly lower.

WHERE TO BUY IT

In this country, there are thousands of places where engagement rings are sold or designed. Nationwide, you can buy from a chain store at a mall, a jewelry salon in a department store, or even from mail-order catalogs. New York City is rare in that you have diamond dealers at your fingertips. Most people who don't have an uncle in the diamond business end up getting a referral from someone who does. But it isn't a guarantee that you'll get dealer prices, or that you'll be dealt with honestly. Says Ted Mandell of New York's Diamond Vault, there's a joke on 47th Street (New York's Diamond District) that more G VS2 diamonds are sold in one year than were mined in Africa in the last hundred, and plenty of them to relatives. The reality is, most people in the United States buy their diamonds at retail. Some stores (namely the fancy boutiques) have a higher retail markup than others.

While getting a good deal is certainly a worthwhile consideration, far and away the most important criteria in choosing a jeweler is that he or she have a reputable, established business with strong ties to the community. You don't want to buy from a fly-by-night operation that won't be there tomorrow. If a store or firm is committed to service and building relationships, it's a good place to start.

With long-standing firms like Tiffany or Cartier, or your local equivalent, all the years in business are signs of professionalism and gem expertise. With newer stores and boutiques, check that a certified gemologist is on staff. The Gemological Institute of America and the American Gem Society certify gemologists, conferring titles of Graduate Gemologist and Certified Gemologist, respectively. Note that getting a certificate directly from the GIA is considerably different from getting an appraisal prepared by a GIA-certified gemologist. Only the GIA certificate is a truly independent and universal declaration of your diamond's characteristics.

Shop around. A diamond merchant who has good prices and nothing to hide can only benefit from couples taking the time to educate themselves. Most feel that at the end of the day, that same education is what will lead you to buy from them.

Better stores will have a reasonable return policy, and often a program for trading in your diamond for a bigger or better one. Ask for this information in writing BEFORE YOU BUY. Reputable stores will be glad to oblige. Shadier operations will hem and haw, or turn you down outright.

When you do purchase a diamond get a detailed description of the ring on the bill of sale. Stores like Tiffany and Fortunoff go one step further and give you a printed certificate detailing all of the characteristics of the diamond. Having a complete description gives you some legal recourse should you discover in the process of appraising the ring for insurance that the ring is not what that jeweler claimed to be selling you.

And remember, if a deal sounds too good to be true, it is.

Your Appraisal

Once you purchase a ring, it's time to get an appraisal.

A solid appraisal is necessary to determine the replacement value of your ring for insurance, and it is your best protection in cases of theft, damage, or loss that the insurance company will provide you with an acceptable quality replacement ring. And it well help verify a ring in relation to what the seller claims.

In looking for a qualified appraiser, consider the following guidelines (suggested by the International Society of Appraisers):

What kind of training, and how many years of experience does he or she have? Look for credentials such as Certified Gemologist Appraiser (CGA), Accredited Senior Appraiser, Certified Appraiser of Personal Property, and titles conferred by various appraisal societies (see Appendix) after an individual has completed programs of study.

Does the appraiser belong to an appraisal organization? Many associations subscribe to ethical codes, that ideally mean customers can feel secure about the appraiser's professionalism and competence.

Will the appraiser supply references? Appraisals are confidential, but with a client's permission, he or she should be able to give you names of recent clients.

What kind of fee schedule does the appraiser have? Most appraisers charge either a flat fee per item, or an hourly rate. Be wary of an appraiser who wants to charge a percentage of the value of your ring. The practice is considered unethical. There's a danger that the appraiser will overvalue your ring, because he makes more money on the deal. If an appraiser proposes this fee method, find another appraiser.

The more detailed an appraisal, the better. A good appraisal contains:

- A very complete description of the mounting, including the weight of the metal and the gross weight of the ring, including the stone.

- A complete description of the stones, including precise measurements of the diamond, its average diameter and depth, table size, and fluorescence, as well as clarity, color, cut, and precise weight of the stone.

- A description of how the stone is set—i.e., channel set, prong set, etc.

- For larger diamonds of ½-carat or above, the appraisal should contain a plot—a map of internal inclusions or blemishes.

One of the most important purposes served by an appraisal is that it gives a well-informed opinion of the average current retail price for that ring in your region. "Remember, an appraisal is an opinion," says Thomas Terpilak, an independent personal property appraiser specializing in jewelry, and a consultant for Metro Gem, a Maryland-based firm.

An appraisal should also be typed on letterhead, not handwritten. A cover letter should list the appraiser's professional credentials. It should also list the grading system used—i.e., GIA, and detail the purpose for the appraisal—i.e., insurance replacement. Appraisals should be updated every few years to reflect market changes in the value of jewelry.

A Note on Insurance

It's in your best interest to see that your ring is adequately covered for theft, loss, or damage. Check with your company to see what their policy is. Despite the fact that you may pay premiums on a $3,500 ring, as valued by your appraisal, in the event that something happens to your ring, most companies will try to supply you with a replacement ring that matches the description of your ring—i.e., a 1-carat H SI stone mounted in gold, as cheaply as possible through their own buying sources. Although some companies do reimburse in cash for cases of value replacement, it's doubly important that your appraisal be complete and accurate.

The Paper Trail

The most important paperwork on your diamond engagement ring is as follows:

1. The bill of sale—it should detail complete information about your ring.

2. GIA certificate—should you choose to get one, this certificate corroborates that what you are buying is what the jeweler (and bill of sale) says.

3. An appraisal—necessary for insurance, a complete appraisal by a qualified individual gives you the information you need to get adequate insurance.

ANTIQUE RINGS

If the ring you want is an antique or period piece, FORGET EVERYTHING YOU'VE JUST READ.

With antique rings, the four C's are not relevant. For starters, the four C's weren't popularized by the GIA until 1953, many years after most heirloom rings were created. More to the point, the value and appeal of antique rings is focused on the setting and the overall beauty of the ring, not the quality of the stones. The mere fact that the ring has survived through the ages also contributes to its worth.

Until the discovery of large mines in Brazil in 1870 diamonds were a rare commodity. By their very scarcity they were considered precious, regardless of flaws. And diamond-cutting techniques were less sophisticated. Many of the antique rings have rose-cut or Old Miner-cut diamonds that reflect light less dramatically than today's brilliant-cut stones with 58 precise facets.

Technically, an antique is anything 100 years or older. The Art Deco and Art Nouveau rings from earlier in this century and the wonderful filigree and engraved rings from the twenties and thirties are referred to as period pieces. In some cases, they are simply called estate rings—which simply means secondhand. While all antique rings are estate rings (worn by a previous owner) not all estate rings are antiques.

What's Available

Most plentiful are rings from the Victorian era and the Art Deco and Art Nouveau periods. Three-stone rings are typical of the Victorian era, as well as the five-stone ring variation. In these types of rings the stones are held in place by delicate scrollwork settings rather than prongs. Some mountings are gold, with scrolls tipped in silver, and in late Victorian years, roughly around 1890, the scrolls are platinum-tipped.

Platinum is a hallmark of Art Nouveau and Art Deco rings. The Art Nouveau rings tend to have flowing, curvilinear shapes, often with a single stone. These rings have a softer look to them than the Art Deco rings, which have strong geometric lines. The Deco rings are the product of an age that gave rise to feats of construction such as the Chrysler Building.

Another popular Victorian style is the cluster ring (think Lady Di's sapphire-and-diamond engagement ring). The jeweler used a single colored stone—such as a sapphire or ruby, and created a ring of diamonds around it, making a flower-like cluster. Occasionally, collectors come across a variation on the cluster ring that has a center diamond, a row of colored stones encircling that, and another ring of diamonds making up the outermost "petals."

It's no surprise that much of the metal work in Deco rings resembles the angularity of suspension bridges rather than the delicate scrolls of nineteenth-century pieces.

Antique diamonds were cut much differently than they are today. Among the popular techniques were rose cuts, Old Miner cuts, and old European cuts. Rose-cut stones come to a point at the top (and, oddly enough, they are flat at the bottom). They have no center table. The faceting arrangement is built around six center facets that make a rose-like shape. These diamonds resemble the beautiful rose stained-glass windows found in stately cathedrals. Old Miner cuts, first seen in the early 1800s, can be quite brilliant and beautiful. They are often described as cushion-shaped, because they are not quite round, but rather are shaped like pillows with rounded corners. Old Miner stones tend to be deep stones. The top facet, known as the table, is smaller than contemporary brilliant-cut stones, and the bottom facet, known as the culet, is larger—ostensibly to let more light through—and they have 58 facets in all. In reality, because of the depth of the stone and the imprecise facets, Old Miner cuts

Inspirations in period platinum: A 1920s diamond solitaire, an Edwardian diamond dinner ring, a 1960s estate ring with an emerald-cut diamond, flanked by step-cut baguettes, and a 1930s Cartier emerald and platinum ring.

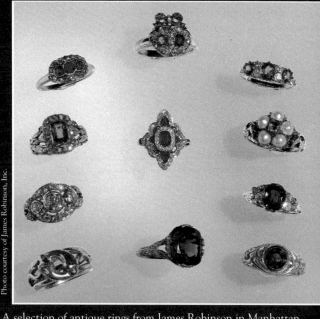

A selection of antique rings from James Robinson in Manhattan. The value and appeal of antique rings is focused on the setting and the overall beauty of the ring, not the quality of the stones. As colored stones were more plentiful and more affordable than diamonds into the early part of this century, antique rings usually feature a colored stone in the center, as in many of the examples pictured here.

are less brilliant, but the small tables afford plenty of fire. Old European cuts debuted in the mid-1800s. These stones have a more perfect round shape, the tables are not quite as small as on the Miners, and the culets are not quite as open. They also have 58 facets.

At James Robinson, a treasure-trove of a store on 57th Street in Manhattan specializing in antique jewelry and silver, Joan Boening and her father Edward Munves sell an extensive selection of top-quality antique rings. According to Boening, the best of what's available in terms of stone quality is a VVS2 stone—as far as she can tell. Boening will not pop a stone from its setting to send it to the GIA for a color and clarity rating, for fear of damaging the setting in the process. And settings can hide imperfections and mask the true color of diamonds. "With old rings you can't be concerned with the four C's. Yes, in a modern ring you want it to be the best it can possibly be, but with an old ring, it's not what makes the value of the ring. You can compare two five-stone rings—one with very large stones and one with very small stones. Yes, the one with large stones will cost more. But you can't compare rings by what the stone is, and what the stone's value is," says Boening.

Buying an Antique

Part of the appeal of antique rings is that they are one-of-a-kind. The craftsmanship in many old rings was wonderful, in terms of detail and construction, and the very care that went into creating the ring has helped it survive through the years. Some rings have been worn more gently than others. Some may have been poorly repaired. When buying an old ring look for quality. Keep the following considerations in mind.

- Has the ring had a hard life or an easy life? Is it in good condition? You can generally tell by examining the ring for wear in the setting and wear to the stones.

- Are the stones badly scratched or abraded? Are there nicks in the sides, or at the bottoms? (Slight nicks might not be noticeable except under a loupe, and might not detract from the beauty of the ring as a whole.)

- Are the stones roughly the same color? If not, it may be an indication that stones have been replaced.

- Is there solder showing on the setting? This is an an indication that the ring has been repaired or that it was sloppily made.

- Do the stones look like they are sitting nicely? Sometimes mine-cut diamonds found in Victorian rings are not cut evenly, and sometimes one table sits up higher in the mounting than another table.

- Does the mounting look bent or misshapen? If so, stones can be easily popped. Or it may be an indication that there is wear in the structure of the mounting, and that it is unsound.

- Are there cracks in the mounting?

- Is the shank of the ring worn thin at the back of the finger?

- Do the prongs look stable and uniform?

- How worn down is the metal holding the stones? Whether it is a channel, bead work, or prongs, metal wears down over time, especially in antique rings— the craftsmen prided themselves in using the tiniest amount of metal possible.

- If under a loupe you see no metal holding the stones, suspect glue. Since the advent of Krazy Glue, people have used glue instead of properly repairing antique pieces. (The glue may be visible from the underside.)

- Is it within your budget?

- MOST IMPORTANT: Is the ring aesthetically pleasing to you?

You might not mind that repair work has been done, or that there is a nick in a stone. It may be part of the one-of-a-kind appeal of the ring. The overriding criterion is that you love it, and that you'll wear and treasure it for a lifetime.

Buying at Auction

One interesting route to owning an heirloom is to buy at an auction house. At a recent Sotheby's Arcade Jewelry auction a 2.84-carat emerald-cut diamond flanked by baguettes and set in platinum went for $4,125. A three-stone diamond and ruby ring with a 1.25-carat antique cushion-shape center diamond set in platinum sold for $2,310. At Christie's East in Manhattan, a Belle Époque ring with an old European-cut diamond set in an engraved platinum mounting recently sold for $3,520. In Manhattan, Sotheby's mounts Arcade Jewelry Auctions every other month, and Christie's East hosts Antique and Fine Jewelry sales in February, April, June, September, October, and December. Additionally, Christie's East sometimes holds special Bridal auctions in June. There are a fair number of antique and estate pieces suitable for engagement rings at these auctions.

If the bidding doesn't get out of hand, it is possible to purchase a ring at auction for good value. At Sotheby's, the catalog estimates for rings are conservative, usually below diamond trade list prices, or at fair market value. Both are considerably less than retail. The average price for an Arcade engagement ring is $5,000. Solitaires start as low as $1,500. Channel-set gemstone band rings start at $800. "At auction, clients have the opportunity to buy a ring without incurring the cost of retail overhead," explains Laura Crimmins, head of jewelry for Christie's East, which also lists rings at fair market value.

Catalogs from the auction houses give an estimate range of what the rings will go for. Although bidding starts slightly below the lower estimate, the estimate is only a starting point. The "X" factor is the bidding process. It's the law of supply and demand. The rings are one of a kind. If there's significant interest in one ring, the bidding moves the price up exponentially. That's the fun (or frustration) of buying at auction.

Tips for Buying at Auction
Jennier Foley, assistant vice president, Sotheby's Jewelry Department, offers these suggestions:

• Try to choose three rings you would be equally satisfied with. If the bidding is fierce on one ring, one of the others may work within your budget.

A selection of antique and estate rings, suitable for engagement rings, from Christie's East December 1992 auction.

- Remember in planning your budget that there's a specific order to every auction. Pieces come up as listed in the catalog. Bid accordingly. If the piece you want most comes up last, you may not want to bid as high on alternate pieces. Bear in mind that there may be competition on any of the rings you want.

- If you have your heart set on a particular piece, plan to be at the auction, or on the telephone when the ring is on the block. By being present you have the option to make a last-minute decision about whether to spend an extra amount—something you can't anticipate when leaving a written bid.

- Use the exhibition as your best learning tool. When buying at auction, you're buying AS IS. The exhibition is your opportunity to get a clear idea of the condition of the ring, the color and clarity, and to learn if there are chips in the stone. The auction house staff is there to inform about quality and suggested bidding. They will also know if a particular ring has been very popular, a barometer of the competition ahead.

APPENDICES

CLEANING YOUR RING

Diamonds have an affinity for oils—the natural lubricants in the skin, hand lotions, and cooking grease, as well as any environmental grit you may encounter. As dirt builds up it dulls your diamond, making it look less bright and smaller. To keep your ring sparkling, it's best to clean your diamond once every month or so. While at-home cleanings are fine for basic maintenance, it's also a good idea to take your ring in for a professional tune-up and cleansing every twelve to eighteen months.

There are as many ways to clean a diamond as there are to make a pie crust. Many of the basic ingredients are the same, but everyone argues their way is the best. Here is a round-up of methods. You choose:

1. You're Soaking in It: The Detergent Bath

Place a few drops of mild liquid detergent in a small bowl of warm water. Immerse ring in suds and gently brush with a soft natural bristle toothbrush. Place it in a wire strainer and rinse with warm running water. Pat dry with a soft, lint-free cloth.

2. The Cold Soak

In a cup or glass, make a half-and-half solution of cold water and household ammonia. Soak for thirty minutes (some say overnight). Remove and tap gently around the back and front of the setting with a small brush. Swish in the solution again, and drain on a paper towel. No rinse is needed.

3. The Quick Spritz

Liberally spray your diamond front and back with Windex. (The main component of Windex is ammonia.) Rinse under warm water. Let drain. (Some caution that if your setting is not pure platinum, or if it is not soldered with a high fineness of gold, the setting will start to oxidize from the ammonia . . . but your diamond will be fine.)

4. Ultrasonic Cleaners

Most experts feel that at-home ultrasonic cleaners are too harsh—particularly on antique pieces, or rings with soft gemstones like emeralds.

Caution: Avoid contact with chlorine bleach when wearing your ring. While it won't hurt the diamond (the word diamond comes from the Greek adamas—*unconquerable or indestructible) it can discolor or create cavities in your mounting.*

RESOURCES

Information Associations

The Diamond Information
  Center
Worldwide Plaza
825 Eighth Ave.
New York, NY 10019
(212) 474-5193
Consumers can write for a free
booklet, *Your Guide to Buying
Diamonds*.

The Platinum Guild
  International
620 Newport Center Drive
Suite 910
Newport Beach, CA 92660
(714) 760-8279
Readers may write to this ad-
dress for information on platinum.

Designers/ Retailers

The designers whose pieces are
pictured in this book will be
happy to refer you to their store
nearest you, or to retailers in
your area that carry their designs.

Aaron Faber Gallery
666 Fifth Ave.
New York, NY 10019
(212) 586-8411

Alexander Primak Jewelry Inc.
2 W. 47th St.
Room 602
New York, NY 10036
(212) 398-0287

Altobelli Jewelers
4419 Lankershim Blvd.
North Hollywood, CA 91602
(818) 763-5151

Bagley & Hotchkiss, Ltd.
5468 Skylane Blvd.
Santa Rosa, CA 95403
(800) 621-4169
(707) 544-8557

Borsheim's
120 Regency Parkway
Omaha, Nebraska 68114
(402) 391-0400

Cartier, Inc.
653 Fifth Ave.
New York, NY 10022
(212) 753-0111

E.B. Harvey & Co.
6191 Bonny Oaks Drive
Chattanooga, TN 37416
(615) 892-2232
(800) 678-4324

Fortunoff
1300 Old Country Road
Westbury, NY 11590
(516) 832-9000

James Robinson, Inc.
15 E. 57th St.
New York, NY 10022
(212) 752-6166

John Atencio
280 Detroit St.
Denver, CO 80206
(303) 322-5581

Mayor's
2352 E. Sunrise Blvd.
Fort Lauderdale, FL 33304
(305) 563-4181

Michael Bondanza
10 W. 46th St.
New York, NY 10036
(212) 869-0043

Nova Stylings, Inc.
6725 Valjean Ave.
Van Nuys, CA 91406
(818) 989-2828

Paul Morelli Design Inc.
132 Chestnut St.
Philadelphia, PA 19106
(215) 922-7392

Paul Phelps
Osborne-Phelps & Co., Inc.
10 W. 47th St.
New York, NY 10036
(212) 719-4130

Reinstein and Ross
29 E. 73rd St.
New York, NY 10021
(212) 772-1901

Richard D. Eiseman
514 Northpark Center
Dallas, TX 75225
(214) 361-0341

Samuel Jewelers, Inc.
17 W. 45th St.
Suite 802
New York, NY 10036
(212) 869-5688
(800) 257-3338

Sam Lehr Designs
35 Harwood Court
Scarsdale, NY 10583
(914) 472-5383

Shreve, Crump & Low
330 Boylston St.
Boston, MA 02116
(617) 267-9100

The Diamond Vault
589 Fifth Ave.
Suite 808
New York, NY 10017
(212) 888-1234

Tiffany & Co.
727 Fifth Ave.
New York, NY 10022
(212) 755-8000

Tivol
220 Nichols Road
Kansas City, MO 64112
(816) 531-5800
(800) 829-1515

Whitney Boin Design Studio
10 Bleecker St.
Suite 1A
New York, NY 10012
(212) 673-0643

William Schraft
58 E. Willow St.
Millburn, NJ 07041
(201) 376-8575

New York Auction Houses

Christie's East
219 E. 67th St.
New York, NY 10021
(212) 570-4830

Sotheby's Arcade
Sotheby's
1334 York Ave.
New York, NY 10021
(212) 606-7000
Readers may write or call for flyers
on upcoming auctions.

Independent Gem Testing Labs

GIA Gem Trade Laboratory
580 Fifth Ave.
New York, NY 10036
(212) 221-5858

International Gemological
Institute (IGI)
580 Fifth Ave.
New York, NY 10036
(212) 398-1700

Appraisal Organizations

Accredited Gemologists
Association
915 Lootens Place
San Rafael, CA 94901
(415) 454-8553
(800) 874-2029

American Gem Society
5901 W. Third St.
Los Angeles, CA 90036
(213) 936-4367
The American Gem Society
will provide information, free of
charge, for consumers interested
in locating AGS jewelers in the
U.S. and Canada. AGS members
are said to subscribe to a
strict code of ethics that prevents
them from misrepresenting
or falsely advertising the quality
and grade of the diamonds and
jewelry they sell.

American Society of Appraisers
P.O. Box 17265
Washington, D.C. 20041
(800) ASA-VALU

Appraisers Association of
America
60 E. 42nd St.
New York, NY 10165
(212) 867-9775

International Society of
Appraisers
P.O. Box 726
Hoffman Estates, IL 60195
(708) 882-0706

National Association of Jewelry
Appraisers
4256 N. Brown Ave.
Scottsdale, AZ 85251
(602) 994-9000

Diamond Price List

The Rapaport Report
15 W. 47th St.
New York, NY 10036
(212) 354-0575